One Step to Bowling
200

Gene Korienek, Ph.D.

Black Dog Innovation, Inc.
Corvallis, Oregon USA

Visit the book site at www.onestepto200.com.

Written by Gene Korienek.

Illustrations by Jimmy Lee Johnson.

Published by
Black Dog Innovation, Inc.
4100 SW Research Way, Suite A
Corvallis, Oregon 97333
USA

Library of Congress Control Number: 2006937465

Printed in the United States of America.

ISBN: 0-9788112-0-8

Preface

So, you bought this book, or perhaps you are standing in a book store right now and wondering if this is THE book to help you become a better bowler. While you're here, let me tell you a story...

A few decades ago when I was 14, and just beginning to bowl in the Junior Leagues in Chicago, IL. I wanted to bowl a 200 game more than anything, but I had serious problems getting strikes, and spares were often a mystery to me. After a few years of bowling in leagues I managed to roll a 200 game. Along the road to bowling my first 200 game I benefited greatly from watching PBA (Professional Bowlers Association) matches on TV. Perhaps the most important piece of knowledge that I acquired from watching the PBA bowlers was the level of consistency required for bowling a 200 score. Looking back at that time in my life I now realize that what I really needed was this book. My message to you is that this is the book YOU need to become a better bowler.

If you are a new or beginning bowler, reading this book will increase your bowling enjoyment and scores by changing the mechanics of how you bowl. It presents an innovative and scientific approach to bowling that makes bowling simpler. It focuses on the 2 most important contributors to higher bowling scores:

1) Accuracy

2) Consistency

This technique trains a beginning bowler to be a human bowling machine able to knock down pins as accurately and consistently as Superman jumps over tall buildings in a single bound. You do believe in Superman, don't you?

You can achieve these results by simplifying the movement of your body while keeping your mind focused on the important aspects of the game. This book teaches you what you need to know about bowling technique. It also treats the Sport of Bowling as a 'Sport' by including simple and focused practice and training regimens to increase your performance and reduce your possibility of injury.

The One Step Approach has been used as an initial learning step in many bowling books but has never been expanded into a legitimate, full scale technique for all bowlers. In this sense, it is a new bowling technique!

Occasionally, a new technique arrives on the scene in a sport. In 1968 high jumping was transformed by the 'Fosbury Flop'. In tennis it was the two handed backhand followed by the two handed forehand. In football it was the conversion from straight kicking to soccer kicking for field goals and extra points. More recently, in baseball it is the drag hitting style exhibited by Ichiro Suzuki.

This book presents a revolutionary bowling technique that will change the way you bowl.

So what is so different about this technique? The answer to this question is: 'Just about everything except the ball!'. As a One Step bowler much of the difficulty of the approach, back swing and release is gone. The primary innovations in this technique are:

1) A One Step Approach.

2) No sliding up to the foul line.

3) A simplified arm swing and release.

4) A simplified targeting strategy.

You will be surprised at how these changes can affect your game and your score. Once you learn this simple bowling technique you will find it to be as natural as pitching a horseshoe or softball.

Actually this movement is very similar to horseshoe and softball pitching. In theory, learning to bowl using the One Step Approach will improve your performance in these sports as well.

This book is small and easy to read. Everything that is discussed in the book is also illustrated in the book. Buy this book, it only costs a few bucks, read it, it only takes a few hours, go bowling, and have fun for the rest of your life.

Gene Korienek, PhD

Personal note to lefties: Those of you who bowl left handed will notice that this book is not written for lefties. That was a decision I made to keep the book as simple to read as possible. I apologize. I am left handed and it pained me to exclude myself. I am considering writing another version of this book that is only for lefties. Go to the web site for the book:

www.onestepto200.com

and let me know what you would like to see.

Until that time us lefties will have to read this book and convert the foot targets, spares, and lane targets to be usable for left handed bowlers.

Acknowledgments

Writing a book always requires a team. The author is the leader of the team but everyone plays the game. In the case of this book there were many people who played on this writing team and I would like to acknowledge their contributions:

The guys I bowled with as a kid who made it an enriching experience, Jim Palka, Tom Samec, and Bob Kasanova.

The management and staff at the Beverly Bowling Lanes in Chicago, Illinois.

My thanks to Ann Asbell, Oregon State University, for letting me present and teach this technique to her students.

Oregon State University students enrolled in the bowling class who were daring enough to try something new, Thanks. Special thanks to Jeremy and Mariam for effort above and beyond normal bowling.

Finally, my thanks to the organizations and people who contributed to the publishing and production of this book:

- Publisher: Black Dog Innovation

- Printer: Lightning Source

- Reviewer: Tom Wrensch

- Illustrator: Jimmy Lee Johnson

As Our Story Begins

Jim, age 14, steps off the Chicago Transit Authority bus into a frigid, blustery, snowy, winter day. It had been snowing forever and there was way too much of the slippery stuff everywhere. As if that was not enough, it was colder than @#**&$#%.

Running and sliding across the street, Jim makes it to the big metal door of the Beverly Bowling Lanes, using 2 hands he swings open the door and reaches the relative safety of the crowded old bowling alley. The change is instantaneous, from freezing cold to comfortable and warm, and from silence to the familiar, and exciting, crashing sound that only a bowling ball can make when crushing a rack of 10 great red and white wooden bowling pins.

Jim is a normal looking kid, not small, not a linebacker, but there is one significant difference in him. Jim wants to be a bowler, he knows it and his friends know it. His mother, of course, has no clue.

Jim, being a frequent bowler in this bowling alley, notices the stranger immediately. He was 20, maybe 50, years old. Jim is not skilled at guessing the ages of older humans. What is immediately apparent is that the old guy seems to be selling books to the people around the registration counter.

Being a curious kid, Jim walks over to see what is going on. He has an hour before his team bowls a match against the infamous league leading Cubbies. The Cubbies are an older, obnoxious, bunch of high school kids. The Sox, Jim's team, has never beaten the Cubbies and there is no reason to believe that record is in jeopardy today.

Jim takes a bold step forward and says, 'Hey fella, can I look at one of those books?' The old guy turns slowly toward him as if he might never make it all the way around, looks at Jim for a moment and says: 'Sure, you look like you might need this book'. While Jim is thinking 'What did that mean?' the old guy pushes one of the small books into Jim's sweaty hands. The book seems to fit his hand perfectly, like an old, well worn bowling glove, but it smelled better. Jim looks at the cover of the book and reads the title: 'One Step To Bowling 200'.

'Holy Batman', he shrieks, 'Is this a bowling book?, he asks everyone in the area.' The old guy, still intently watching him, answers his question with a simple 'Yes, of course, would you like one?'.

Jim was a bit overwhelmed. Here was a bowling book in his hand and he had no money to buy it. The old guy seems to look right through Jim's head and stares deeply into his dilemma.

'Hey Kid, you're Jim, right?'

Jim perked up and reflexively stepped back. That seemed like a pretty normal question, but, he wonders, 'how did this guy know my name'?

'Well, my Mom calls me Jim but my Dad sometimes makes up other names for me, like Jimbo or Dumbo.'

'I thought it was you, happy to finally meet you', mumbles the old guy. 'What do you think of the book?' Jim begins to page through the book and look at the pictures. The people in the illustrations are bowling, but it seems somehow simpler than bowling as Jim knows it. The title promises that the reader would, could, should bowl a 200 game if he, she, or it reads this book. This was too much to pass up.

'I want one!' Jim sneezed. He, and just about everyone in Chicago has a cold. Except, strangely, the old guy. Actually, the old guy has a suntan. Strange.

'Okay', says the man and he holds out his hand for the money.

'OOPS', said Jim. 'I don't have any money.'

The old guy gave Jim one of those adult smiles, kind of like Jim's teachers, and says, 'Tell ya what, I will GIVE you one of these books, if you and the rest of your teammates read it and try out the new bowling technique described in the book.'

Jim hears the word 'GIVE' and immediately says the word 'OKAY'. He slowly turns and begins to walk away, glancing furtively behind him as if he thinks he is taking advantage of the old guy. He stops and takes one last look and says, 'What's your name?'

The old guy responds: 'My name is Gene, enjoy the book'.

Jim walks, as if in a daze, to the dark corner of the bowling alley over by the pool tables where the really old guys hang out and smoke cigars. He finds a seat, sits, and stares at the cover of the book as if he does not quite know what to do with it. Time slows as Jim begins to read. It is not like a school text book. It is easy to read and there are so many illustrations he can almost understand it without reading. He finds himself consuming every word as if it was a piece of candy. He can't stop. He goes on and on through the technique part and on to the part about how to get more strikes when he hears his teammate say: 'Jimbo, we gotta bowl now. Hey, what are you reading?'

'I'll tell you later' he yells as he runs to the lane, hops over the ball return and plops into a seat next to his teammates. Jim thinks, 'I wonder if this book will help us beat the Cubbies?'

And that is the end of this little story... or, perhaps, it is the beginning of a much bigger story?

Read on, Jim!

PART
I

One Step to Bowling 200

The Technique

PART I

The Technique

Introduction

This part of the book is where you actually learn the One Step Approach to bowling. Read through the technique step by step. There are illustrations of bowlers for each step. Study the illustrations, they will probably tell you as much about the technique as the writing.

Bowling is deceptive. When you first learn about it, it seems easy, but after a while you begin to realize that it is actually quite difficult. The difficulty emerges when you realize that, in order to bowl a good score, 200 for example, you must be very accurate again and again. In other words you must be consistent.

What keeps bowlers from consistently being accurate? Where do errors come from?

In a conventional bowling approach, you walk forward from a starting point on the lane to a stopping point at the foul line while you develop your arm swing. The difficulties in the conventional approach involve walking accurately to your foul line target, managing your arm swing while you are walking and linking the timing of your arm swing with your walking. That's a complex series of activities, and complexity produces errors.

In the One Step Approach you are not walking toward the lane while swinging a bowling ball at your side. You are simply standing and taking one step. This results is a much simplified arm swing resulting a tighter synchronization and better performance.

Simplicity produces consistency!

The One Step Approach

Like most things, the One Step Approach has a sequence of activities. The list below shows the activities you have to complete. The rest of this chapter will describe each step in more detail with illustrations showing how to do it right.

1) Pick up your ball.

2) Get your mind ready to bowl.

3) Get your body ready to bowl.

4) Find your targets.

5) Push out the ball.

6) Let the ball swing back.

7) Let the ball swing forward.

8) Throw the ball onto the lane.

9) Release the ball.

10) Evaluate your performance.

Good Luck!

Pick up your ball

There is a preferred way to pick up and handle a bowling ball. It has to do with taking care of your bowling hand. When bowling, your hand must hold on to a heavy object, swing that object around, and eventually throw it down the lane. Save your hand for bowling. Do not carry your ball around with your fingers inserted in the ball. Carry the ball as shown in the illustration to the right.

Important: Your non-bowling hand is supporting the weight of the ball and your fingers are not in the ball until you are actually ready to bowl.

It is very important to establish consistency in your approach to bowling. If you watch professional athletes in any sport they all have a ritual that they go through prior to action. In baseball a batter may adjust his hat or knock non-existent dirt from his spikes prior to assuming his batting stance. We see the same phenomenon in the Basketball free throw, Tennis serve, Baseball pitch, Golfing putt, and other skill based activities. All athletes who must perform consistently begin their performance with a ritual and a consistent starting posture. This is the beginning of your ritual.

Check list:

1) Pick up the ball with 2 hands

2) Carry the ball cradled in your non-bowling hand

3) When you get to your starting location on the lane, place your non-bowling hand under the ball and insert your fingers into the ball.

4) Rotate the ball in your hand until your bowling hand is on the right side of the ball and your fingers are inserted in the ball.

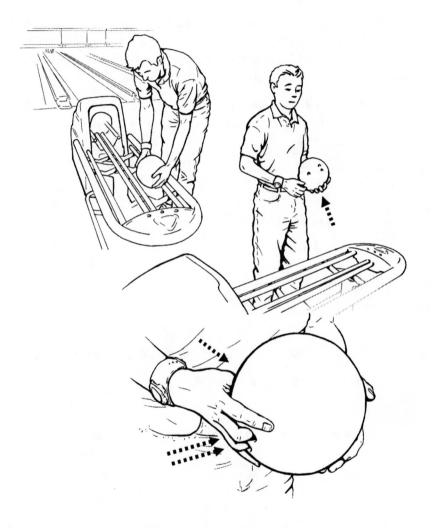

Pick up your bowling ball

Get your mind ready to bowl

For the most part you bowl with your mind. If your mind is not ready to bowl your body will be confused about exactly what to do and it will make errors resulting in you not getting that strike you want. It is VERY important for you to get your mind focused on the task of getting a strike, nothing else.

You must have a mental ritual that you go through prior to starting your bowling movement. Do the items on this check list prior to every shot:

Check List:

- ✔ Close your eyes.
- ✔ Visualize your last shot.
- ✔ If it did not hit the 1-3 pocket:
    - ✔ Identify the problem.
    - ✔ Determine how to fix it.
    - ✔ Tell yourself what you are going to do.
    - ✔ Visualize your upcoming shot as a perfect strike.
- ✔ Hold the ball at waist height.
- ✔ Look at your lane target.
- ✔ Smile. Everything is easier when you smile.

You are now mentally ready to bowl.

Your mind is ready to bowl

Get your body ready to bowl

In any sport the starting point and posture are critical. Because of the accuracy and consistency required in the sport of bowling, the starting spot and posture have even more impact on performance. All bowling approaches start with the bowler moving to a start position holding the ball. The One Step Approach places additional focus on this early component of the bowling approach because consistency and accuracy are stressed.

Okay, now pick up your bowling ball and assume your bowling posture. If you are at home learning from this book then walk to a part of the room and assume your bowling posture. It will help if a friend is there to compare your posture with the posture shown in the illustration to the right. If your posture does not look the same as this illustration, fix it. If you have no friends, stand in front of a mirror and look at your posture.

Compare what you look like in the mirror to what the bowler in the illustration on the next page looks like. You and the illustrated bowler should have the same posture. Use the check list below to guide your assessment.

Check List:

    1) Foot Placement & Balance

    2) Head & Eye Position

    3) Posture

    4) Left Arm Position

    5) Right Arm Position

    6) Ball Height

Your body is ready to bowl

Find your targets

There are three very important targets that you must find when you step up to the lane:

Starting Target - Position yourself one step from the foul line. For most people one step will be about 3 feet. Take your time and experiment to find a comfortable step length. Initially, position your left foot so it is in line with the center dot on the approach. After you determine the amount your ball hooks you may want to move your left foot target several boards to the right.

Step Target – Your step target will be a point a few inches from the foul line. Do not step on the foul line. The step target should be straight ahead of your start target.

Ball Target – A good beginning ball target is between the second and third arrows from the right channel (gutter). As you determine the amount your ball hooks you will find that your ball target will be about 6 to 10 inches to the right of your foot target. Keep in mind that your ball target moves right or left as your foot target moves right or left.

Important: You may move your foot target right or left on the lane but you should always step straight toward the pins, not at an angle. Your step, arm swing, and ball release should be straight down the lane and to the right of the center dot to allow your hook to hit the strike pocket. As shown in the illustration to the right, your ball will hook to the left. Your task is to determine the amount of hook and move to the right enough to have your ball hook into the 1-3 pocket.

There are several factors that affect the amount of hook your ball will have: grip, lane conditions, ball speed, and the amount of lift, or ball spin, you generate in your release.

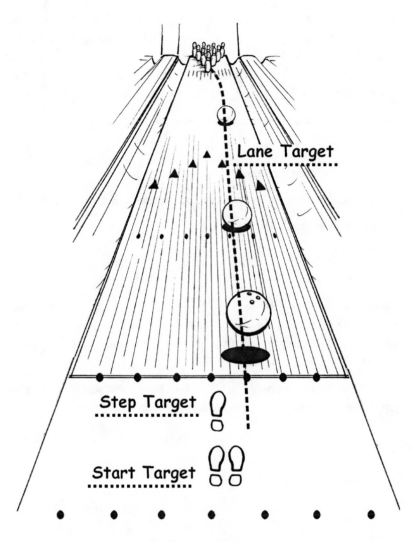

Find your targets

Create your Arm Swing

The arm swing is the core of your bowling technique. At this point in your delivery you are mentally ready to get a strike. You are in your bowling posture. You are standing upright, not bent over at the waist. The ball is supported by your left hand placed under the ball. Your fingers are comfortably inserted in the finger holes of your bowling ball but not supporting its weight.

The arm swing has four main components:

1) Push the ball out.

2) Let the ball swing back.

3) Let the ball swing forward while taking a step forward.

4) Throw the ball onto the lane.

5) Release the ball.

About your Step – Make the length of your step comfortable. Make sure your step foot lands close to the foul line but not on or over it. Stepping on the foul line is a 'foul' and the outcome of the ball you throw will be zero.

Initiate you step forward as the ball moves forward past your hip. Your step should be completed as the ball is being released.

Push the ball out in front of you to your chosen target height. Your target height will be something that you choose but it should be near shoulder height. Pushing the ball out higher will result in a higher back swing and more ball speed.

Push the ball out

Let the ball swing back as your arm swings down and past your hip. The ball should rise approximately to the level of your shoulder in the back swing.

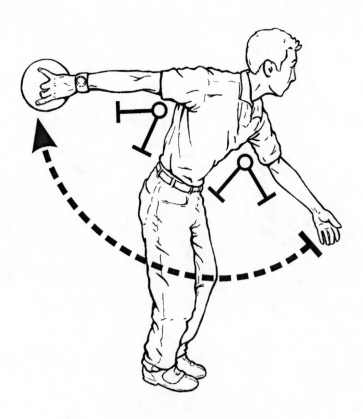

Let the ball swing back

Let the ball swing forward toward the foul line, take a step forward to your step target, and bend your left knee a bit to facilitate your balance and lower the ball to the lane. Begin to take your step as the ball comes forward. Your step should be completed at the same time the ball crosses the foul line.

Let the ball swing forward

Throw the ball onto the lane

The throw begins when the ball hovers at its highest point in your back swing. At that point the ball is stationary. A lot of important stuff happens at the beginning of the throw. Notice the height of the back swing, a higher back swing will result in increased ball speed. Notice also that there is no step forward at this time. Following that, the ball begins to come down from the height of the swing, picking up speed, moving at its highest speed just as it crosses the foul line during your release.

The Step forward begins when the ball begins its flight down from the top of your back swing and begins to move forward. The forward movement of the ball is then matched by the forward movement of your step. You move your center of mass forward as the center of mass of the ball moves forward. Think of you and the ball as a single mass moving forward together.

You begin your step as the ball moves forward. You will know when to take your step, it will seem natural and necessary to step forward to prevent yourself from falling over. Make your step a natural walking length. When your foot lands at the foul line, bend your knee to maintain balance and to bring the ball down to a few inches above the lane.

The throw ends at the point of release. When and how you make that release will impact your effectiveness as a bowler and your ability to get strikes.

The ball should roll over your lane target on a track parallel to the lane boards. It is important that you throw the ball straight toward the pins and not at an angle. If your arm swing is moving in a straight line toward the pins then your ball will also.

Throw the ball out onto the lane about 1 foot past the foul line. Do not drop it on the line. A hand towel placed on the bowling lane just past the foul line will help you to train yourself to loft the ball about 1 foot past it.

Step forward and throw the ball onto the lane
(Side View)

Step forward and throw the ball onto the lane
(Back View)

Release the ball

You release the ball just after it goes past its lowest point in your arm swing. The timing of the release is critical.

If you release it too soon you will drop the ball either before or on the foul line. If you drop the ball you lose control of where it will go. You will also not be able to impart any spin on the ball and therefore will not be able to throw an effective hook.

If you release it just right you will actually throw it out onto the lane past the foul line. A well thrown ball will land about 1 foot beyond the foul line.

Hand Position

the hand position shown below is for a hook ball. Notice that your hand is on the side of the ball and your wrist is stiff and straight.

 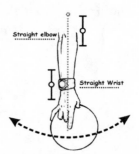

If you release the ball too late it will bounce out onto the lane and you will wind up off balance.

Evaluate your throw performance

- Look at where your ball rolled over the target
- Look at the angle of throw
- Observe the speed
- Observe the hook

The Release

Evaluate Your Performance

Yes, it is true, you must keep score, but in today's newer bowling establishments scoring is done for you automatically. Your game score is called an outcome measure. It is a measure of the outcome of your effort. However, your bowling score is not all there is to bowling. It tells you how many pins you knocked down but does not tell you much about your performance.

I suggest that you keep two bowling scores. The first is your game score. The second score is your performance score. Your performance score is more important because it actually evaluates how WELL you bowled as opposed to what SCORE you bowled. Your teammates or your bowling league will record your scores and update your average. You will have to maintain a bowling log that contains your performance scores. There is a performance score sheet in the appendix of this book.

The score sheet includes:

- Number of times you hit the 1-3 pocket.
- Number of times you hit the 1-3 pocket and make a strike.
- Number of times you missed the head pin.
- Keep track of what spares you leave, particularly the following:
  - Light in the pocket
    - 5 pin
    - 5-7 pins
    - 2-4-5-8 pins
  - High in the pocket

- 4-7 pins
- On the head pin
  - 7-10 pins
  - 4-7-10 pins
  - 4-7-6-10 pins

If you are bowling well you should not get spares other than the ones I listed. Keep in mind that your objectives are:

1) Hit the pocket on the first ball.
2) Make the easy remaining spare with the second ball.

Good Luck!

PART

II

One Step to Bowling 200

Getting Strikes

PART II

Getting Strikes

Introduction

What is a strike, really? How does one bowling ball knock down ten pins? Well, it all starts 60 feet from the head pin when you release the ball.

As your hand and the ball cross the foul line, your thumb begins to come out of the ball, your hand continues to move forward and up. This motion causes your fingers to impart spin on the ball to lift it out onto the lane spinning and sliding toward your lane target.

The ball is traveling at about 19 mph (28 fps) toward an inevitable collision with the 1 - 3 strike pocket. The weight of the ball, the speed it is traveling, and the angle of attack created by the ball hooking toward the pocket combine to create a chaotic spattering of pins all over the pin deck as the ball drives its way through to the end of the lane.

While the pins are knocked down the ball is also deflected as it makes it way through the 10 pins. The maximum weight of a bowling ball is 16 pounds. The weight of 10 pins is 35 pounds. The collision is formidable.

The illustration to the left shows the typical path of the ball going through the pins, resulting in a strike.

A strike ball hits between the 1 and 3 pins. As it moves through the pins it is deflected onto a path similar to the illustration below.

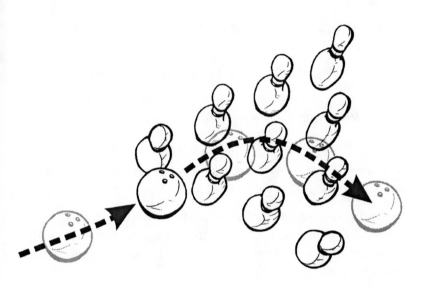

The path of a strike

Your objectives in bowling are to get as many strikes in a row as possible and knock down any remaining spares. In order to do this you must learn to consistently put your bowling ball in the strike pocket. As you may know there are many ways to get strikes. Getting a strike is not a precise thing, but then neither is sinking a putt or a free throw. The four most important things to consider when trying to get a strike are:

1) **Accuracy**: Putting the bowling ball in the 1-3 strike pocket.

2) **Consistency**: Putting the ball in the pocket more often than not.

3) **Momentum**: Throwing a powerful ball.

4) **Angle of attack**: Throwing a hook or a curve

If you are consistently throwing a high momentum ball accurately into the strike pocket you will get a lot of strikes.

Knowing how to consistently throw an accurate, powerful strike ball is something you have to learn but it is also useful to diagnose what went wrong when the outcome of your attempt does not result in a strike.

Accuracy

The most important skill in bowling is accuracy.

If you can put the ball where you want it, you have a job as a professional bowler. But, unfortunately, if you look at all forms of athletic behavior you will see pitchers missing strike zones, tennis players hitting nets, and golfers missing the holes.

A good bowler is an accurate bowler. A REALLY good bowler is a REALLY accurate bowler. Bowlers acquire bowling accuracy through simplifying their bowling movement, staying focused, and combining practice with more practice. Keep in mind that bowling is something you do *in* competition. Practice is something you do to improve your performance *before* competition.

In the field of Sport Psychology there is a concept called the *Practice Effect*. The practice effect says that performance of a skill will increase with practice. More practice means better performance. There are more factors involved in improving accuracy, namely attention, expectations, prior learning, fitness, and fatigue but practice will train your mind to focus your attention, manage your expectations, and erase prior learned bad habits.

Practice is only effective if you evaluate the outcome of each ball you throw. Good and bad bowlers make mistakes. Good bowlers learn from their mistakes by understanding what they did right and what they did wrong every time they throw the ball onto the lane. They then use this information, called feedback, to modify and improve their next attempt to throw the ball.

The feedback that is most useful has to do with your performance rather than your outcome. For example, if you throw a ball that misses the pocket go through the following checklist of your technique to find out where the error came from:

✔ Starting target – Did you start at the right foot target?

✔ Push out – Was your push out at your intended height?

✔ Step target – Did you step to your step foot target?

✔ Back swing – Was your back swing height correct?

✔ Release – Did you release the ball correctly?

✔ Lane target – Did the ball roll over your lane target?

✔ Ball speed – Was your ball speed what you wanted?

The four most common errors are:

1) You made a step error and your step foot missed your step target at the foul line.

2) You made a release error by not having the correct hand and wrist position or you dropped the ball at the foul line rather than lofting it over the foul line to impart spin on the ball to make it hook.

3) You made a push out and/or back swing error. The height of the back swing which in turn determines the speed of the ball. If your ball hooked past the pocket you may have thrown the ball too slow. If the ball did not make it to the pocket you may have thrown the ball too fast.

4) You simply were not paying attention. You had a focus failure. It happens to the best of bowlers. Being focused is not easy but you can learn it. Actually you MUST learn it if you want to consistently throw strikes.

For a right handed bowler the most effective strike ball goes between the #1 and #3 pins. Look at the pin diagram shown on the left.

The thickest line has the greatest likelihood of creating a strike. The thinner lines will generate strikes sometimes but not consistently. Ball tracks shown as thin lines may leave you with a 1, 2, 3, or 4 pin spare.

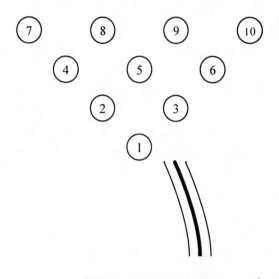

Ball path and pin diagram

Consistency

The objective of the One Step Approach is to increase the percentage of pocket hits in a game. The simplicity of the approach and the straight ahead targeting method WILL increase your consistency.

Consistency is different from accuracy. Accuracy is about how accurate you were when you threw your last ball. Accuracy is measured in inches. Consistency is measured in the percentage of time you were on target.

Consistency of performance comes from consistency of movement. Bowling is a simple sport, the pins are consistently in the same place. Despite this, consistently hitting the pocket is not an easy task.

Consistency starts with:

1) State of mind. Focus.

2) Foot placement at starting foot target.

3) Foot placement at step foot target.

4) Push the ball out to begin arm swing.

5) Control the height of the back swing.

6) Loft the ball onto the lane a foot past foul line.

7) Roll the ball over the lane target.

Item #1 is about focus and attention.

Items #2,3,7 are about hitting the targets and putting the ball where you want it.

Items #4,5 determine the speed of the ball. Be consistent

Items #6,7 determine the hook of the ball. Be consistent

Momentum

Ball Weight - A bowling ball weighs much more than any other object you throw or roll in your day to day activities, typically between 8 and 16 pounds. Most beginning and intermediate bowlers throw a ball that is too heavy for them. They are motivated to get strikes and think that a heavier ball will help. For some bowlers that will be true but for most bowlers it is not. What is true is that ball weight is a part of ball momentum and is an important component of a *powerful* ball. A powerful ball is one that drives through the pocket creating a condition where pins are being pushed off the lane by both the ball and the other pins.

I suggest that, if you are a healthy adult, begin with a 10 or 12 pound ball. If you are a younger bowler, an older bowler, or an injured or disabled bowler use a lighter ball. The thinking behind these decisions is that you must be able to control the ball in order to put it in the pocket. A ball that is too heavy for you will control you and you will never reach your potential as a bowler.

Using a lighter ball will let you focus on your technique. As you begin to consistently hit the pocket, you can choose to go to a heavier ball, but continue to monitor the results. If going to a heavier ball is reducing your performance, go back to the lighter ball.

If you truly think that a heavier ball will give you more striking power, use the training techniques described in the Coaches Corner of this book to strengthen your hand, arm, and shoulder before you attempt to use a heavier ball.

Go to the local pro shop or bowling center to get a personal, professionally fitted bowling ball. It will make a BIG difference in your bowling.

Ball Speed - Beginning bowlers often try to throw the ball too hard, thinking that more ball speed will knock down more pins. Once again, throwing the ball hard is not a good way to get more strikes. Typically, a ball speed at release of less that 20 fps is considered slow, 20 to 28 fps is average, and greater than 28 fps is considered fast.

Creating this speed consistently using muscular force would be difficult. Rather than use muscle to create the speed and direction of the ball, good bowlers take advantage of gravity and an effective arm swing.

In the One Step Approach the speed of the ball comes solely from your arm swing. For the most part, the speed of the ball is determined by how high you push the ball out in front of you when you start your bowling movement.

You can directly measure the speed of your bowling ball traveling down the lane with a watch, though a stopwatch will be more accurate.

A bowling lane is 60 feet long from foul line to head pin and the formula to calculate speed is: Speed = Distance / Time. If it takes your ball 3 seconds to go the length of the lane (60 feet) then your ball speed in feet per second (fps) would be: 60ft / 3sec. = 20 fps. Keep in mind that this is the average ball speed not the actual speed of the ball when it hits the pins. The friction of the ball in contact with the lane reduces the ball speed as it travels down the lane.

There is a time versus speed table in the appendix that will help you calculate your ball speed.

Angle of Attack

What is angle of attack? Well, if you are throwing a straight ball from the middle of the lane directly at the pins you would have an angle of attack of zero degrees.

Why is angle of attack important?

First of all, it is only important to getting strikes. If you throw a hook your ball will start out going straight down the lane and then make a hook, or turn, toward the strike pocket. The purpose of the hook ball is to alter the angle of attack in an attempt to reduce the deflection of the ball when it hits the pins.

The amount of deflection is a matter of angle of attack and momentum.

When the ball hits the 1-3 pocket it will be deflected away from the pins, which could leave some of the interior pins standing because the ball was deflected away from them. Increasing the angle of attack reduces the deflection of the ball when it strikes the pins. This in turn allows the ball to drive through the pins more effectively.

This diagram illustrates a strike ball being deflected as it enters the 1-3 strike pocket:

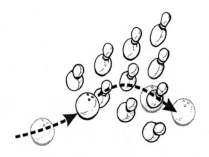

PART

III

One Step to Bowling 200

Making Spares

PART III

Making Spares

Introduction

Every strike you make is one less spare that you have to pick up. As you know, the fundamental law of the One Step Approach is to hit the strike pocket every frame. With this in mind, and some effort and practice on your part, you will not be looking at many spares. What you want to do in any given game is to see more strikes than spares on your score sheet.

'The best strategy for making spares
is to make more strikes.'

Strategy

First, there are 4 important things to remember when trying to make spares:

1) Make strikes to reduce the number of spares you leave.

2) Put your ball in the strike pocket to reduce the variety of spares you leave. You will not always get a strike just because you put the ball in the pocket, but you will at least get a spare that you are good at picking up.

3) Practice the spares that you are most likely to leave and become VERY GOOD at picking up those spares.

4) Rule of Thumb - Never miss more than 2 spares a game if you want to bowl a 200 game.

Second, your mental focus is the most important part of picking up spares. Learn and use the following process to create a focus that will put you on track to picking up any spare you may leave: ·

1) Know where to start on the lane, where to step, and where your lane target is.

2) Visualize the ball crossing over you lane target and hooking into the spare.

3) Verbalize to yourself what you are about to do.

Now that I have said that, lets talk about how to make the spares you will leave when you fail to get a strike. The illustrations on the following pages will show you the foot, step, and lane targets for the most common spares you might leave. In general:

1) Use as much of the lane as you can

2) Stay away from the channels (gutters)

3) If you throw a big hook, consider minimizing it to make getting a spare simpler.

Light Pocket Hit

The illustration below shows the ball deflection on a light hit. On a light pocket hit you could possibly leave the:

- 5 pin
- 5-7 split
- 2-4-5 mini bucket
- 2-4-5-8 dinner bucket

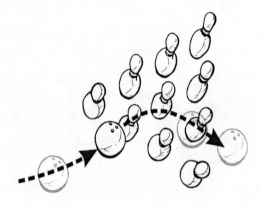

The illustrations on the following page will show you three important pieces of information necessary to pick up spares:

1) Your starting foot target

2) Your step foot target

3) Your lane target

A light pocket hit, one that does not hit the head pin full enough, may result in leaving the 2-4-5 cluster of pins, the 5 pin or the 5-7 mini split.

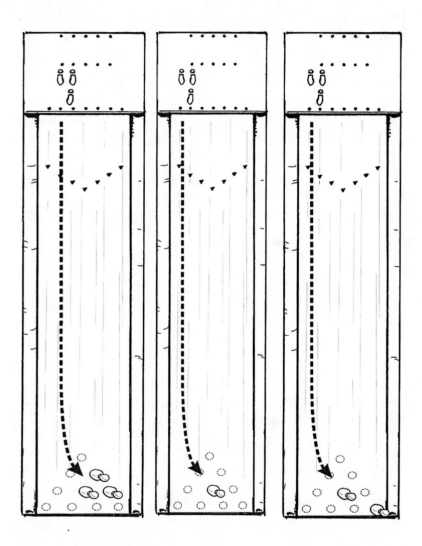

Pocket Hit

The illustration below shows the ball deflection on a pocket hit as the ball travels through the pins. In this case you will either have the strike that you've always wanted, or you could possibly leave the 10 pin. Leaving the 10 pin, in this case, is often referred to as a 'tap'.

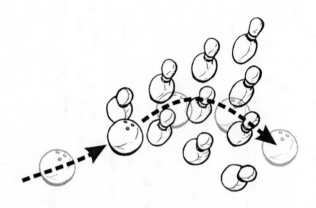

The illustrations on the following page will show you three important pieces of information necessary to pick up spares:

1) Your starting foot target

2) Your step foot target

3) Your lane target

Sometimes a pocket hit will, sadly, leave a 10 pin. Get over it and hit the 10 pin as shown. Notice that, unlike other throws in the One Step Approach, you are throwing the ball diagonally across the lane. This diagonal throw will reduce the likelihood that you will throw the ball into the channel (gutter).

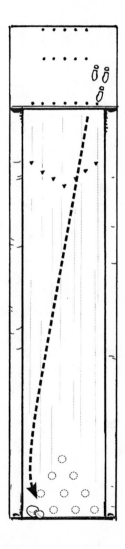

High Pocket Hit

Getting a high pocket hit means that you were close to the optimal strike pocket but you hit too much of the head pin. As a result, you left one of the following pin combinations:

- High 4 pin
- Very high 4-7 pair

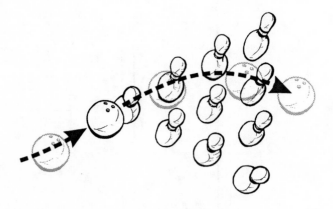

The illustration on the following page will show you three important pieces of information necessary to pick up spares:

1) Your starting foot target
2) Your step foot target
3) Your ball target

When the ball hits high in the pocket, you will often leave the 4 pin. If it hits higher in the pocket you will likely leave the 4-7 pins. In either case you pick up the pair in the same way.

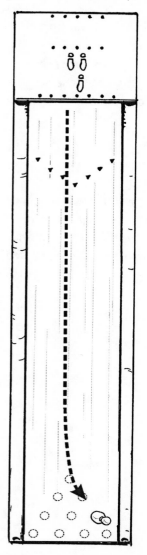
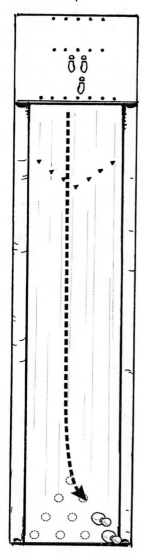

On the Head Pin

If you hit directly on the head pin or close to it you may wind up with a split. Splits are an unfortunate outcome of hitting directly on the head pin. Some bowlers actually practice converting splits. I strongly suggest you practice converting the spares you will see most often. Do not even bother practicing splits, it is a waste of time. Use the start, step, and lane targets shown below and pick up as many pins as you can. The most common splits are:

- 7-10 split.
- 4-6-7-10 split.

The illustrations on the following page will show you three important pieces of information necessary to pick up the 7-10 or 4-6-7-10 split. Do not let it raise false hopes, it is not likely that you will convert this split, but your teammates will be impressed if you do.

The strategy that I would like to suggest when confronted with splits is to knock down as many of the remaining pins as possible. For example, in the 7-10 split knock down one of the pins, as a right handed bowler, it will be easier for you to knock down the 7 pin. If you are confronted by the 4-6-7-10 split use the same lane target to knock down the 4 and 7 pins. Good luck.

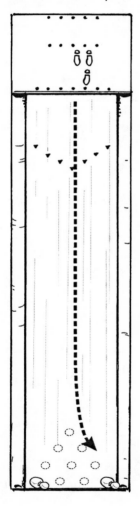

Part IV

One Step to Bowling 200

Coach's Corner

PART IV

Coach's Corner

Introduction

The coach's corner is something new. It was designed to be a lot like a conversation between a bowler and a coach. In this case, the bowler is our fictional friend, Jim and the coach is the author of this book. This does not substitute for a real coach. A personal coach will accelerate your growth as a bowler. If you cannot find a coach you then this may be the next best thing.

The coach's corner addresses issues you may have with your bowling performance. Jim, the character from the story in the front of this book of this book, asks the Coach questions about bowling and the Coach answers. Read through it. You may find that often Jim is in need of the same information as you.

1) K.I.S.S. Principle

2) Focus

3) Bowling Equipment

4) Where do errors come from?

5) Practice

6) Warming up

7) Ball Speed

8) Striking Power

9) Making Spares

K.I.S.S. Principle

Coach: Before we get started, let's discuss the two most important objectives of a good bowler:

1) Accuracy

2) Consistency

Jim: OK, coach but how do I become more accurate and consistent?

Coach: I suggest using the **K.I.S.S.** principle or 'Keep It Simple, Stupid'. It seems to work well wherever it is applied. NASA uses it in design reviews. Baseball players use it in thinking about their swing.

The One Step Approach to bowling is a K.I.S.S. approach.

It is designed to be simple because when something is simple it becomes repeatable. This means that you can do it over, and over again, and receive about the same results. Every time you walk onto a bowling lane and step up to your starting point you want your bowling movement to have about the same results, a 1-3 pocket hit and, hopefully, a strike.

The One Step Approach helps to keep bowling simple because:

1) There is only 1 step rather than 3, 4, or 5.

2) It is easy to finish your approach with your foot on your target every time because there is only 1 step and no sliding at the foul line.

3) The timing between your arm swing and your approach is much simpler because the approach is simpler.

4) The differences between rolling for a strike or a spare are simple changes in your starting spot and your lane target. Everything else is the same.

Focus

Jim: My bowling is getting slowly better but I still have problems consistently throwing the ball over my lane marker. How can I be more consistent?

Coach: Well, Jim, practice will help in the long run, however there is something that you can do NOW that will impact your bowling performance NOW.

Jim: What can I do?

Coach: Focus your attention on your bowling. For example, imagine that you are getting ready to bowl. What is your mind doing while you are getting ready to bowl?

Jim: I don't understand. What do you expect me to do?

Coach: If you are like most people, your mind is always thinking of something. When you are bowling you mind has to be focused on your bowling. Be methodological. Be detailed. Be consistent.

I expect you to go through your 'ready to bowl checklist' in your mind to prepare yourself for the next frame of bowling in the same sense that an airplane pilot goes through a preflight check list. Here is your checklist:

- ✔ Pick up your ball.
- ✔ Walk to your foot target.
- ✔ Face the pins.
- ✔ Stand upright, no bending at the hip.
- ✔ Hold the ball next to your right hip.
- ✔ Smile to yourself (Much of life is about state of mind.)
- ✔ Look at your lane target.
- ✔ Push the ball out to your target height.

- ✔ Let it swing back.

- ✔ Let it swing forward.

- ✔ Throw the ball onto the lane.

- ✔ Watch it roll over your lane target.

- ✔ Evaluate your performance.

If you are not thinking like this you have already made an error and do not know it. The potential for an error on your next shot is increasing.

Start out right, right now!

Bowling Equipment

Jim: **HEY, COACH!** What is the best bowling ball weight for me?

Coach: Nice to see you are reading the book and have gotten this far Jim. Most bowlers, particularly strong bowlers, will pick the heaviest ball available to them, 16 lbs. For many bowlers that could be a mistake. Keep in mind that I think bowling is about putting the ball in the strike pocket. Because of that, I recommend throwing a lighter ball for better ball control while still maintaining enough ball momentum to carry your strikes.

Jim: Yes but, all my friends throw heavy balls and throw them fast.

Coach: There is a tendency to pick a heavier ball, throw it harder, and generate a stronger hook to get more power on your ball in order to broaden your strike zone. These ball selection and style strategies can be effective for highly skilled bowlers. They are often not so effective for beginners, intermediates, or less skilled bowlers. In the One Step Approach accuracy and consistency are paramount. Keep these items in mind when picking a ball:

1) Your considerations for a ball are different when using the One Step Approach. You are not carrying the ball while walking down the approach any more. You are standing in one spot and taking One Step.

2) Choose a ball that is a few pounds lighter than you are used to and move to a heavier ball as you become more comfortable throwing for accuracy. You will carry strikes because of your accuracy more often than your speed and power. This is true for novices and professionals.

3) Experiment with balls of differing weights from 6 to 16 Lbs. Use the one you can control the best. Remember bowling is not about how hard you throw or how heavy the

ball is, rather it is about accuracy and consistency.

One more thing for you to think about, Jim, is that the weight of the ball really only makes a difference when throwing a strike ball. Weight, speed, hook, and other factors will have different effects on your spare game. Often the decisions a bowler makes to improve his/her strike game, like speed, ball weight, and exotic grip may make picking up spares more difficult. Keep that in mind when you are making ball and grip choices.

Jim: Thanks Coach! While we're talking about bowling ball selection, what grip should I use?

Coach: Good question, Jim. Without going to any of the exotic grips you have three basic grip choices. Let's discuss the grips according to how much of each finger you put in the ball.

- **Full finger grip** - Full thumb in the ball with 2 fingers in the ball up to the 2nd digit. This is the standard grip used by most beginners and some intermediates.

- **Semi-finger tip grip** - Full thumb in the ball with 2 fingers in the ball up to the 1st digit but with the fingers not fully extended. This grip will require more wrist and grip strength.

- **Full-finger tip grip** - Full thumb in the ball with 2 fingers in the ball up to the 1st digit with the fingers fully extended. This grip requires a lot of wrist and grip strength.

When you are talking with the professional at the bowling center the choices you have to make when you choose a grip will determine:

1) **Ball control** – resulting in you consistently hitting your lane target.

2) **Lift** - resulting in revolutions on the ball as it moves down

the lane.

3) **Release** — resulting in your being able to consistently release the ball at the correct wrist angle, with a consistent lift, and at the correct point in your approach.

Any of the grips listed above could work for you. The question is which is the BEST for your capabilities and style. It comes down to knowing the trade offs of the different grips and making an informed decision.

The *best control* of the ball comes from the full finger grip. It gives you the most secure hold on the ball; however it does not give you the lift that a semi-fingertip or full fingertip grip has to offer.

The *best lift* will come from the full fingertip grip because the lifting point, the fingertip, is farthest from the thumb. This is the least secure of the three and requires the most hand strength to maintain a firm grip.

I suggest starting with a full finger grip and transitioning to a semi finger tip grip when it seems like the right step to take.

Jim: Do you think I should get a wrist support?

Coach: The purpose of a wrist support is to establish a stable forearm to hand angle so that when you release the ball at the foul line you are consistently doing it with the same forearm to hand angle. With no wrist support you must maintain hand position with muscular effort. Consistent hand position is critical to consistent release which is critical to consistent strike pocket hits. I recommend you try out one of the wrist supports for sale in your local pro-shop. You will need to bowl more than 3 games over a few days to determine if wrist support is what you want.

Jim: What about a bowling glove?

Coach: The purpose of a bowling glove is to provide a firmer and more supported grip on the ball. A firmer grip on the ball will have a positive impact on your control. It will also facilitate your holding and releasing the ball.

I strongly suggest the use of a bowling glove. There are wrist supports that are also bowling gloves. I think this kind of combination product makes sense.

Jim: How do I choose a pair of bowling shoes?

Coach: When using a conventional, 3, 4, or 5 step approach you are traveling at about 3 MPH when you arrive at the foul line. You have to reduce this speed to zero in order to stop. Bowling shoes have a leather surface on the foot opposite the hand you use to throw the ball. If you are right handed your left foot will slide 3 to 6 inches up to the foul line. The leather sole will allow you to come to a sliding stop to facilitate your maintenance of balance.

In the One Step Approach you do not walk up to the foul line, you are already there. You are taking one step. Your body mass is moving forward and is stopped when you put your foot down on your target at the foul line. In the One Step Approach you will not be sliding or shuffling your feet. You will not be walking. You will simply be taking One Step. Because of this, the soles of your bowling shoes both need to be made from a non-sliding, preferably rubber material. A rubber, rather that leather, sole will promote a firm and consistent foot plant that will reduce variability.

That said, you could use a comfortable rental shoe and not experience any difficulties because the shoe is not very critical in the One Step Approach. Bowlers using the 3, 4, or 5 step approach will benefit from a good pair of shoes because the slide at the foul line is critical to the termination of their approach.

Jim: Thanks. I am off to the pro shop to do some shopping.

Where do errors come from?

Jim: Coach, Where do errors come from?

Coach: Jim, once you know how to bowl and you have thrown a strike by correctly using your technique, any deviation from your correct technique will likely result in an error.

The source of errors is YOU and only YOU can make the changes needed to get rid of an error. Whenever you feel that you are making errors go back to the basics. Go over this list and go back to the illustrations depicting correct bowling form and technique.

Foot Placement

Walk to your spot on the lane and place your left foot on your starting spot. Be exact. If necessary, use a felt tip pen and make a mark on the tip of your bowling shoe to help you to put your foot exactly on your spot every time. Look at the foot placement dots on the lane and use one of them as a guideline.

Balance

You should feel comfortable and stable in your bowling stance. Notice that the placement of your right foot is a bit different. Look back at the illustration 'Getting your body ready to bowl', and place both feet as shown. This is important because you want to place your feet to give you the most stability. Keep your center of mass over your right foot. Do not lean or sway to the right, left, front, or back.

Head Position

Your head should be pointing directly toward the pins. Keep it steady before, during, and after you throw the ball down the lane.

Eye Position

Your eyes need to find the target at the foul line where you are going to place your foot after you complete your One Step. Once you are comfortable that you, can and will, place your foot on your foot target at the end of your step, stop looking at it.

From this point on your eyes should be looking at the lane target that you are going to roll your ball over, nothing else. All during your arm swing and throw your eyes should see only your lane target. You should see only the lane target and nothing else.

Posture

Your posture is basically upright with no bending at the waist. Your knees are slightly bent so that they are not locked.

Left arm position

Your left arm should be bent about 90 degrees at the elbow with your palm facing up and holding the ball.

Right arm position

Your right arm should also be bent about 90 degrees at the elbow. Your right hand should be on the right side of the ball with your fingers comfortably inserted in the finger holes of the ball. Put your thumb in first, followed by your fingers.

Ball height

Hold the ball at about waist height on the right side of your body so that when you begin your arm swing the ball will swing past your hip without a problem.

Jim: Thanks Coach!

Practice

Jim: Hi Coach! I need some advice on practice. I seem to be slowly improving. I want to get better, faster. Will practicing help me?

Coach: Yes, practicing will help your game. Actually it is very important for you to begin practicing NOW. If you wait too long you will begin to improve your bad habits rather than improve your game.

Jim: How do I get started?

Coach: Keep in mind that *You bowl with your brain.* Does that sound strange to you? I hope not because the basis of practice is that you are training your brain to be very good at repeating your best bowling movement.

There are several forms of practice that you can use to improve your game.

1) **Mental Practice** – Mental practice is my personal favorite. It is practice that you do in your head. Because you are not actually getting your body involved, you can do this kind of practice relaxing in your most comfortable chair or while lying on the beach. You simply imagine yourself bowling correctly. Use your bowling check list. Visualize yourself picking up your bowling ball and walking to your starting spot on the lane. Assume your starting posture. Look at every part of your body to verify that it is in the right position. Look at your imaginary lane marker and visualize yourself going through your bowling movement. In your visualization you do it perfectly and get a strike.

   Visualize the details of your bowling movement and always visualize a perfect strike.

2) **Modeling** – Modeling is another way to practice. It

involves performing you bowling movement at home with a friend watching you and acting like your coach. You could also do your movement in front of a mirror. Once again be very critical, focus on the details, and try to make your bowling movement better with each attempt. Modeling should be done without a ball.

3) **Physical Practice** - Physical practice means you are actually on the bowling lane, practicing your bowling. To get the best results from this type of practice Set up a practice schedule that has you throwing two games:

   a) One game of throwing strike balls to increase your ability to hit the strike pocket.

   b) One game throwing at spares you are most likely to leave as a result of a thin or high pocket hit.

When you practice you get better. This change in performance is called the *Practice Effect*. There are 2 types of practice schedules.

The first is called a *Massed Practice Schedule* because you are focusing your practice on a particular, single, aspect of your game and repeating that several times in a row. Practicing 20 strike balls in a row is massed practice.

The second is called a *Distributed Practice Schedule* because you are mixing different bowling activities. For example, a distributed practice would consist of bowling a game because a conventional game is a mixture, or distribution, of strikes, and spares.

Finally, the last thing I have to say about practice is called the *Specificity Principle*. This principle says that you will improve a specific skill by specifically practicing that skill.

Jim: Sounds kind of obvious.

Coach: Yes, it does when you hear it, but people often practice things that are not specific elements of the bowling movement. Make sure you practice those skills you want to improve.

Jim: Okay, I will put together some practice schedules. Thanks.

Warming up

Jim: Hi Coach! I am ready to bowl.

Coach: Are you, Jim? Before performing any exercise, it is important to warm up your muscles. Bowling is no different from any other sport in this respect. While bowling may seem to be a relatively low level exercise, the repetitive nature of the sport, and the necessity to carry and deliver a weighted ball can be significant exercise. It is possible for the muscles and joints to be strained if they are not well prepared.

During bowling, repeated strain is put on various areas of your body, particularly your shoulder, arm, wrist, and knees. Also, many muscle groups are involved in the bowling action, including the forearms, shoulder, back, torso, hips and legs.

In any sport, the specific training exercises performed should include the body parts that are being used, and should take you at least through the range of motion that is required.

Your warm up should be done before each bowling session. A walk around the block would be about the right level of activity to increase blood flow to the muscles and get your body ready to do some bowling.

The best measure of warm up is heart rate. A heart rate of about 125 is generally considered to be the ready to exercise heart rate. You can monitor your heart rate by lightly placing your index finger on one of the arteries showing on your wrist. Pick a spot where you can feel pulse, count the number of pulses for 15 seconds and multiply that number by four. The answer is your heart rate in beats per minute.

Passive Stretches

Once you are warmed up you need to stretch the muscles you will be using to bowl so they will be flexible and more resistant to injury. Hold each of the following stretches for 10-20 seconds and go through the series of stretches three times.

Neck Stretch – Tilt your head forward until it touches your chest and you can feel tension at the back of your neck. Tilt your head left and right slowly until you feel the stretch.

Shoulder Stretch 1 - Point your elbow upwards, with your hand behind your head. With your other hand grab your elbow and gently pull towards the other side until a good stretch is felt. Repeat for both arms.

Shoulder Stretch 2 - Hold your arm horizontally across the front of your body. With your other hand, grab your elbow and gently pull towards your chest. Repeat for both arms.

Side Stretch - Begin in a similar position to **Shoulder Stretch 1** above, with feet slightly apart. Keeping your hips stable, bend your torso so that the stretch is felt along your side. Do for both sides.

Leg Stretch 1 - With your body and feet facing forward, place one leg back and your other leg forward, put your hands on your front thigh. Shift your weight forward remaining as upright as possible and keep both feet flat on the floor. Repeat for other leg.

Leg Stretch 2 - Support yourself with one hand while standing on one leg. Bend your free leg back and hold on to your ankle with your free hand. To increase the stretch, pull your foot higher behind your body.

Forearm Stretch 1 - Hold out your arm with your palm facing down. Relax your wrist and let your fingers and palm point downward. Grab your fingers with your other hand and pull them towards your body. Do for both arms.

Forearm Stretch 2 - Hold out your arm with the palm facing up. Relax your wrist and let your fingers and palm point downward. Grab your fingers with the other hand and pull them down and towards your body. Do for both arms.

Ball Speed

Jim: Coach, I see a lot of people throwing the ball pretty fast. Is that what I should do?

Coach: The best speed for your ball is the one that works best for you. In general, the best speed for knocking down bowling pins is in the range of 20 feet per second (fps) to 28 fps. Ask a friend to help you measure your ball speed by using a watch or, better yet, a stopwatch to measure the amount of time that passes from the moment you release the ball until it hits the pins. Since the lane is 60 feet long, if your ball takes 3 seconds to get to the pins then it is traveling at 20 fps.

A ball speed less than 20 fps is considered too slow to consistently carry a strike. A ball speed more than 28 fps is considered too fast and likely to knock pins off the deck too quickly thus reducing pin action and the likelihood of a strike.

A simple formula for calculating the speed of your bowling ball as it travels down the lane is:

Formula: Speed = Distance / Elapsed Time

Example: 25fps = 60ft / 2.4s

Because you are throwing a hook ball, the slower you throw it the more it will hook. Because of the dynamics of the hook, accurate speed control is very important to accurate bowling.

In the One Step Approach the ball speed is primarily set by the height of the back swing. The back swing is modified by the height of the push away. You have 2 opportunities to control speed:

1. Raising or lowering the height of your back swing will raise or lower your ball speed.

2. If you are not generating enough ball speed using the above mechanism, you can begin to accelerate the ball on

the down swing using your shoulder muscles.

Using option 1 will provide the most consistent speed control. Option 2 will offer higher ball speeds but it also forces you to regulate the speed of the ball with muscle power.

Jim: Okay, so the more consistent approach to controlling ball speed is to control the heights of the push out and back swing.

Coach: That is correct Jim. Take a look at the next three illustrations. The first shows a bowler with a low push out and back swing. This bowler will be throwing a rather slow ball.

Slow Speed

Using the Height of the push out to control ball Speed

This is an example of pushing the ball out higher. This action will cause a higher back swing and result in a higher ball speed.

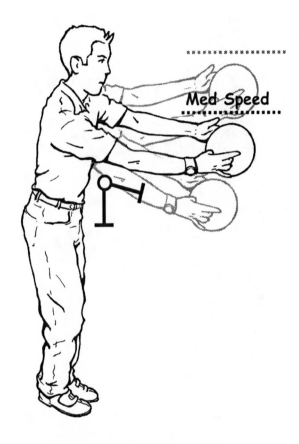

Med Speed

**Using the Height of the push out
to control ball Speed**

This bowler is pushing the ball out much higher and will produce a higher back swing and high speed ball.

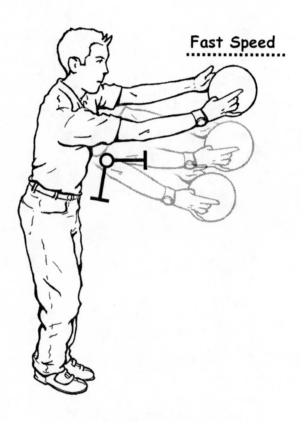

Fast Speed

**Using the Height of the push out
to control ball Speed**

Jim: That was really helpful. So, the higher I push out the ball, the higher my arm swing will be.

Coach: Yes, within limits, that is how it works. The illustration below shows different back swings the the slow speed back swing highlighted.

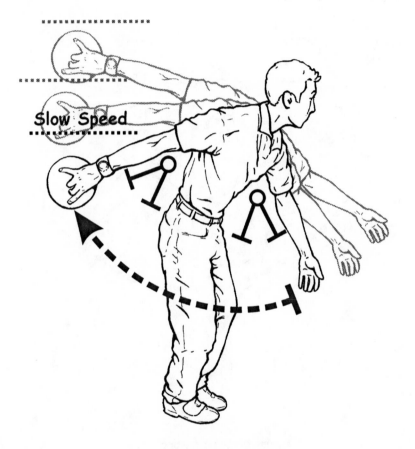

**Low back swing produces
a slower ball speed**

The following illustration shows a medium height of back swing that will produce a medium speed ball.

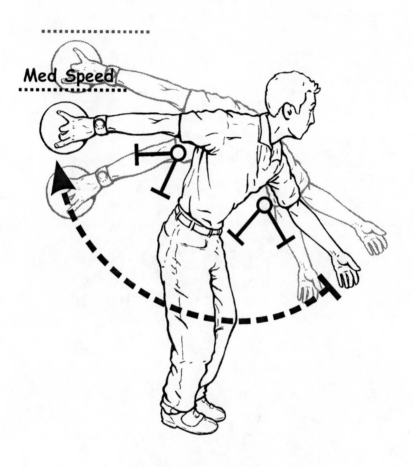

Medium back swing produces
a medium ball speed

This illustration shows a high back swing and will produce a high ball speed. Notice that the height of this back swing is just above shoulder height. This is about as high as you want to go. A back swing that is greater than shoulder height may result in lack of control and accuracy.

**High back swing produces
a high ball speed**

Striking Power

Jim: **HEY COACH!** How can I increase my striking power?

Coach: Everybody asks me this question and my answer is always *'You are asking the wrong question'*. Accuracy and consistency are much more important than power.

Jim: Yes but, all my friends are talking about striking power.

Coach: I know, Jim. As I said in the equipment section of the coaches corner, ball weight, ball speed, and angle of attack all impact striking power. If you do not have the striking power you are looking for then experiment with a heavier ball, or throw the ball faster, or perhaps re-drill your ball for a different grip. Moving from a standard grip to a semi finger tip grip will usually give you a bigger hook and an increased angle of attack. If you are a beginner or intermediate I would not recommend making changes until you are comfortable with your technique.

Jim: So what do I do?

Coach: Think in terms of what works best for you. Keep in mind that your objectives are to:

1) Hit the strike pocket.

2) Make any remaining spares.

The assumption here is that even if you hit the strike pocket you may not knock down all 10 pins. There are many reasons why a ball thrown in the pocket may not produce a strike. Two of the more important reasons are ball momentum and angle of attack, both of which we talked about in the **PART II - Getting Strikes** section of this book.

As a beginning bowler you must think of your growth as a bowler the same way you would think of climbing a set of stairs. Make initial decisions and evaluate them each time you take a step up the stairs.

Jim: Yes, but I want to improve my scores.

Coach: I understand. You want to improve your bowling skill and that is what you should focus on, not your scores. As your skill improves your scores will also.

Jim: Okay, what I really want to do is to throw my ball into the strike pocket. Right?

Coach: Right! The best way to more consistently put your ball in the strike pocket is to practice throwing strikes. I suggest practice games. A practice game is a game where you are throwing just strike balls. Every time you step up to the lane throw your strike ball.

Jim: Hmmm... practice specific shots in order to improve in those specific shots. Thanks Coach, I'm going to practice!

Making Spares

Jim: Coach, I am hitting the head pin about 7 times a game and the strike pocket about 5 times a game and getting better. My problem is that I am missing most of my spares. It is not because they are difficult, I'm just missing them.

Coach: The first thing you need to think about is that '*the more you hit the strike pocket, the easier spares you will leave*'. The second thing is to practice the spares you are most likely to leave. Do not practice spares that are unusual. Focus on those spares you will probably leave in a game.

Jim: How will I know what spares to practice?

Coach: That is easy, I will tell you. Keep in mind that a spare is basically the outcome of what you did when you threw your first ball in the frame. If you did very well, you have no spare because you got a strike. If you hit the pocket but were a few boards off you either hit too much of the head pin or not enough of the head pin. Hitting too much of the head pin is often called being high in the pocket, while hitting too little of the pocket is often called being thin in the pocket.

Jim: What happens if I am too high in the pocket?

Coach: High in the pocket will leave a 4 pin or a 4-7 combination. The approach to making these two spares is about the same. If you make the 4 you will come very close to making the 4-7.

Jim: What happens if I am too thin in the pocket?

Coach: If you hit the pocket a bit thin you will leave a 5 pin, a 5-7, or maybe a 2-4-5. It is also possible that you will leave a 2-4-5-8. If you practice making the 2-4-5 you will also be practicing the 2-4-5-8 because the approach to making both of these spares is basically the same.

Jim: What happens if I am way too high in the pocket or I hit the head pin directly?

Coach: In general, the higher or thinner you are the more pins you are going to leave and the more complex spare you will have to make. In the case where you hit the head pin directly or almost directly, you may leave what is called a split. There are a variety of splits, none of which are easy to pick up. I suggest if you are looking at a split do not bother trying to pick it up. Go for the best pin count and move on to the next frame.

Coach: Before you go Jim, the important thing is to practice those spares that you will be seeing in an actual game.

I suggest a practice session that involves throwing 3 balls at each spare and 5 balls at the 10 pin conversion. Do this each time before you bowl in your league.

This session will be just one game. Because you are just throwing at spares, you do not care if there are pins standing. For example, if you are practicing the 4 pin conversion then throw your first ball at the 4 pin, whether you hit it or not, throw your second ball at the 4 pin also.

Appendices

The appendices of a book are generally reserved for additional items that help the reader understand what was written in the book. In this case, I am putting some small items in these appendices that might be helpful to you.

1) Bowling check list
2) Strike Practice Schedule
3) Spare Practice Schedule
4) Ball Speed table
5) Performance Evaluation Form

Bowling Check List

Memorize this check list. Go through it every time you throw a bowling ball.

Pick up your ball

Walk to your foot target.

Check List:

- ✔ Pick up your ball.
- ✔ Walk to your foot target.
- ✔ Face the pins.
- ✔ Stand upright, no bending at the hip.
- ✔ Hold the ball next to your right hip.
- ✔ Smile to yourself (Much of life is about state of mind.)
- ✔ Look at your lane target.
- ✔ Push the ball out to your target height.
- ✔ Let it swing back.
- ✔ Let it swing forward.
- ✔ Throw the ball onto the lane.
- ✔ Watch it roll over your lane target.
- ✔ Evaluate your performance.

Strike Practice Schedule

Bowl one game using both your first and second balls in each frame to throw strike balls. This means that you will throw between 10 and 20 strike balls. Focus on the details each time you throw the ball. Pay particular attention to:

1) Foot Target

2) Step Target

3) Lane Target

4) Ball release

5) Ball speed

Pay attention to each of the following each time you throw the ball:

- Did the ball go over lane target? If it did not go exactly over the lane target, how much did it miss by. 1 board? 2 boards? Record how accurate you are in throwing the ball over your lane target.

- Was the ball lifted out onto the lane? Did it have the right amount of spin? Did it hook about right?

- How the ball speed? Did you push out the ball to the right height? Was you back swing at the right height?

- Did you step on your step target?

Spare Practice Schedule

The spares that you need to practice are those that you leave when you hit the pocket but do not get a strike. These spares will be determined by where your ball hits the pocket. The possibilities are:

1. Light pocket hit

2. Pocket hit

3. High pocket hit

This means that you will be practicing converting each spare either three or five times as determined by the practice session shown below. Keep in mind that we are assuming that if you hit the pocket you got either a strike or a 10 pin.

Practice Session (This practice session is basically 1 game as recorded by the bowling lanes.)

Light Pocket Hit

> Do each three times: 5 pin conversion
>
> 2-4-5 cluster conversion
>
> 5-7 split

Pocket Hit

> Do five times: 10 pin conversion

High Pocket hit

> Do each three times: 4 pin conversion
>
> 4-7 cluster conversion

If you hit directly on the head pin you may leave a split. You may also get a strike. Strange things can happen! In any case do not practice converting splits.

Ball Speed Table

Ball speed should be measured in feet per second (fps), miles per hour (mph) are included for comparison. The optimal ball speed is between 20 and 28 fps. Use the following table to help with your ball speed measurements:

SEC	FPS	MPH
1.0	60.00	40.91
1.1	54.55	37.19
1.2	50.00	34.09
1.3	46.15	31.47
1.4	42.86	29.22
1.5	40.00	27.27
1.6	37.50	25.57
1.7	35.29	24.06
1.8	33.33	22.73
1.9	31.58	21.53
2.0	30.00	20.45
2.1	**28.57**	**19.48**
2.2	**27.27**	**18.60**
2.3	**26.09**	**17.79**
2.4	**25.00**	**17.05**
2.5	**24.00**	**16.36**
2.6	**23.08**	**15.73**
2.7	**22.22**	**15.15**
2.8	**21.43**	**14.61**
2.9	**20.69**	**14.11**
3.0	**20.00**	**13.64**
3.1	19.35	13.20
3.2	18.75	12.78
3.3	18.18	12.40
3.4	17.65	12.03
3.5	17.14	11.69
3.6	16.67	11.36
3.7	16.22	11.06
3.8	15.79	10.77
3.9	15.38	10.49
4.0	15.00	10.23

Performance Evaluation Form

While your bowling score is what every one will look at and will determine whether your team wins or loses. Your actual performance is measured in a different way.

Your performance is determined by your ability to consistently:

1) Step on your step target.

2) Push the ball out to the correct height.

3) Create a back swing of the correct height.

4) Lift the ball out onto the lane.

5) Maintain a consistent ball speed.

6) Roll the ball over your lane target.

You can evaluate your performance by keeping track of:

1) Number light pocket hits / game.

2) Number of pocket hits / game.

3) Number of high pocket hits / game.

4) Number of strikes / game.

5) Count the number of times you leave each of the following spares:

Leave	Probable cause
1) 10 pin	Pocket hit
2) 5 pin	Light pocket hit
3) 5-7 split	Light pocket hit
4) 2-4-5 cluster	Light pocket hit
5) 2-4-5-8 bucket	Light pocket hit
6) 4 pin	High pocket hit

7) 4-7 pins   High pocket hit

8) Other splits   Something went wrong

I think you should keep a little black book in your ball bag to record this kind of information. Create a table that looks something like this:

Date:	
Spare	**Times Left**
10	
5	
5-7	
2-4-5	
2-4-5-8	
4	
4-7	
Split	
Strike	

Draw this table in your little black book and put a mark in the 'times left' column for each time you leave a particular spare or get a strike.

A

Action
>Is the movement of the pins when the ball hits them. A slower ball with a lot of action will leave moving pins on the pin deck to knock down other pins. A slow ball with high pin action can be more effective than a fast ball with little action.

Addressing the pins
>The bowler's stance just before the approach.

Alley
>A group of lanes or the bowling establishment that houses them. Is sometimes used to mean a single lane.

Angle of attack
>The angle at which the ball is traveling when it hits the pocket.

Approach
>The bowlers movement from addressing the pins to completion of delivery.

Arrows
>Seven marks on the lane that provide a target for the bowler to aid in determining the correct path for the ball.

B

Baby split
>A split with a relatively small space between the pins. The

2-7 or 3-10 splits are considered baby splits.

Backup

A ball that breaks backward: to the right for a right hand bowler or to the left for a left hand bowler.

Ball return

The track and mechanism that returns the ball from the pit.

Ball track

A region or track on a lane where most balls are rolled.

Body english

Useless body movements intended to coax or steer the ball as it moves down the lane. Completely ineffective unless it works.

Brooklyn hit

Hitting on the wrong side of the headpin: the left side for a right-handed bowler and the right side for a left-handed bowler.

Brooklyn strike

A strike from a Brooklyn hit.

Bucket

Leaving the 2-4-5-8, 1-2-3-5, or 3-5-6-9 pins.

C

Channel

The politically correct name for a gutter.

Choke

To do poorly in an important situation because of nervousness.

Clothesline

Leaving the 1-2-4-7 or 1-3-6-10 pins.

Convert

To make a spare.

Count

The number of pins knocked down by the first ball in a frame.

Cross-over

A ball that crosses the head pin to hit the Brooklyn pocket.

Curve

A ball that has a large, slow break. Usually thrown toward the channel and curves back to the pocket.

D

Delivery

A bowler's entire movement including the follow-through.

Dots

Marks on the runway and lane that guide the bowler's approach and throw.

Double

Two consecutive strikes.

F

Fingertip grip
> A grip in which the fingers are inserted only as far as the first joint.

Five-bagger
> Five consecutive strikes.

Flat ball
> A ball with little or no spin. Produces little or no action.

Follow-through
> Technically, the bowling arm continuing to move up after the release of the ball. Can be used to mean all the bowler's movements to the final post-throw posture.

Foul
> Crossing or touching the lane past the foul line during delivery. Pins knocked down after a foul are not counted.

Foul line
> A red line between the end of the approach and the beginning of the lane. The foul line is 60 feet from the head pin.

Foul detector
> A device that sets off an alarm when the bowler crosses the foul line.

Four-bagger
> Four consecutive strikes.

Frame

One of ten parts of a bowling game.

Full hit

Hitting the head pin at or near the center. Often results in a split.

G

Gutter

A depressed area on either side of the line which guides the ball to the pit if it leaves the lane. The politically correct term for gutter is 'channel'.

Gutter ball

A ball that leaves the lane and ends up traveling down the gutter.

H

Handicap

An adjustment made to a bowler's score to help equalize competition.

High hit

A pocket hit that hits too much of the head pin.

Higher

Farther to the left.

Hook

A ball that breaks sharply toward the pocket. A hook changes the angle of attack to improve the chance of a strike.

House ball
A ball provided by a bowling center, as opposed to a ball owned by the player.

K

Kingpin
The 1-pin.

L

Lane
The playing area excluding the gutters and approach. The lane is 42 inches wide and 62 feet, 10 3/4 inches long.

Leave
The pins that remain after the first ball in a frame.

Lift
Upward motion provided by the fingers during release. Additional lift increases the spin on the ball.

Light hit
A ball that hits less of the head pin and more of the 3 pin.

Loft
The distance the ball travels between release and hitting the lane.

Lofting
The act of throwing the ball onto the lane as opposed to rolling it onto the lane.

Low

Describes a thin hit.

M

Mark

A spare or strike, so called because of the x or slash mark put on the score sheet rather than a number of pins.

Miss

Same as open.

Mixer

A ball with a lot of action.

N

Nose hit

A ball that hits directly on the head pin. Often results in a split.

O

Open frame

A frame in which the bowler doesn't get a strike or spare.

Open bowling

Bowling for the fun of it versus competing in a league or tournament.

P

Perfect game

A score of 300, requires getting 12 consecutive strikes.

Picket fence

Leaving the 1-2-4-7 or 1-3-6-10 pins.

Pin deck

The area of the lane where the pins stand.

Pit

The area just past the end of the lane.

Pocket

The space between the head pin and the 3-pin for right-handed bowlers, and the 2-pin for left-handed bowlers. This is the target for the first ball in a frame.

Pushaway

The start of the approach, when the bowler pushes the ball away from the body.

R

Range finders

Marks on the lane that help the bowler determine the target or are used as the lane target. There are two sets, ten dots seven feet past the foul line and seven arrows in a triangle 16 feet beyond the foul line.

Release

The time and position at which the bowler releases the ball. Also refers to the hand action that takes place at that time.

Rotation

The spin on the ball that creates both the break and action of the ball.

S

Spare

Knocking down all of the pins in a frame with the second ball. The score for the frame is 10 plus the number of pins knocked down with the first ball of the next frame.

Spare leave

The pins standing after first ball is rolled, but often used to mean a leave for which it is relatively easy to get a spare.

Split

A leave for which the remaining pins are widely separated, making a spare difficult. The 7-10 split is the most difficult to convert.

Spot bowling

Using a target on the lane rather than the pins as an aiming point. For example, many bowlers use the range finders.

Strike

Knocking down all ten pins with the first ball of a frame. The score for the frame is 10 plus the total number of pins knocked down by the next two throws.

T

300 game
>A perfect game.

Track
>A worn or dry area on a lane that tends to guide the ball to the pocket.

Triple
>Three consecutive strikes.

Turkey
>Three consecutive strikes (same as a triple).

Turn
>The motion of the hand and wrist at release that cause the ball to spin.